Good Advice from Bad Women

by

Carly Herriges

720 – Sixth Street, Box # 5
New Westminster, BC
V3C 3C5   CANADA

Good Advice from Bad Women

Title: Good Advice from Bad Women
Author: Carly Herriges
Publisher: Silver Bow Publishing
Cover Design: Candice James

All rights reserved including the right to reproduce or translate this book or any portions thereof, in any form without the permission of the publisher. Except for the use of short passages for review purposes, no part of this book may be reproduced, in part or in whole, or transmitted in any form or by any means, electronically or mechanically, including photocopying, recording, or any information or storage retrieval system without prior permission in writing from the publisher or a licence from the Canadian Copyright Collective Agency (Access Copyright).

www.silverbowpublishing.com
info@silverbowpublishing.com

Library and Archives Canada Cataloguing in Publication

Title: Good advice from bad women / by Carly Herriges.
Names: Herriges, Carly, 1994- author.
Description: Poems.
Identifiers: Canadiana (print) 20190117648 | Canadiana (ebook) 20190117699 | ISBN 9781774030448
  (softcover) | ISBN 9781774030455 (HTML)
Classification: LCC PS3608.E77 G66 2019 | DDC 811/.6—dc23

ISBN: 9781774030448 (print)
ISBN: 9781774030455 (eBook)

Good Advice from Bad Women

These poems are inspired by the daring, dangerous and sometimes diabolical women throughout history.

DISCLAIMER These poems in no way are meant to memorialize or justify any crimes or heinous acts committed by any subject in any way.

Dedicated to all of the dangerous women I have loved and lost. You have taught me most of all.

Good Advice from Bad Women

Good Advice from Bad Women

Table of Contents

Anne Bolen Teaches Patience ... 9
Elisabeth Bathory Teaches Self Care ... 10
Lizzie Borden Teaches Getting What You Want ... 11
Madame Alexe Popova Teaches Sisterhood ... 12
Ma Barker Teaches Motherhood ... 13
Virginia Hill Teaches Priorities ... 14
Moll Cutpurse Teaches Confidence ... 15
Tituba Teaches Acceptance ... 16
Rose O'Neal Greenhow Teaches Loyalty ... 17
Salome Teaches Revenge ... 18
Anne Bonney and Mary Read Teach Friendship ... 19
Mary Tudor Teaches Conviction ... 20
Calamity Jane Teaches Storytelling ... 21
Peggy Shippen Arnold Teaches Staying Humble ... 22
Catherine The Great Teaches the Value of a Good Education ... 23
Belle Starr Teaches Power Plays ... 24
Pearl Hart Teaches Personal Freedom ... 25
Jezebel Teaches Faith ... 26
Delilah Teaches Honesty ... 27
Beulah and Belva Teach the Price of Fame ... 28
Cleopatra Teaches Politics ... 29
Bonnie Parker Teaches True Love ... 30
Mata Hari Teaches the Power of Sexuality ... 32
Mary Mallon Teaches Passion ... 33
Eve Teaches Blame ... 35
Joan of Arc Teaches Sainthood ... 36
Lady Godiva Teaches Body Positivity ... 37
Emily Hobhouse Teaches Feminism ... 38
Amelia Earhart Teaches Fearlessness ... 39
Silvia Pankhurst Teaches Forgiveness ... 40
Boudica Teaches Retribution ... 41
Mary Shelley Teaches Inspiration ... 42
Marie Antoinette Teaches Apology ... 43
Artemisia Gentileschi Teaches Art Appreciation ... 44
Ching Shih Teaches Achievement ... 45
Abigail Adams Teaches Democracy ... 46
Grace O'Malley Teaches Confident Mindset ... 47
Florence Nightingale Teaches Cleanliness ... 48

Marie Curie Teaches Anatomy of a Superhero ... 49
Clementine Delait Teaches Certainty ... 50
Lucille Ball Teaches Bossiness ... 51
Hedy Lamarr Teaches Being Too Much... 52
Lozen Teaches the Art of War ... 53
Nellie Bly Teaches Investigative Journalism ... 54
Bettie Page Teaches Single Girl Lifestyle ... 55
Irena Sendlerowa Teaches How to Swim ... 57
Christine Jorgensen Teaches Rolling with The Punches ... 58
Lilith Teaches Demonology ... 59
Khutulun Teaches Physical Education 60
Elizabeth I Teaches How to Be alone ... 61
Lela Lombardi Teaches Driving Lessons ... 62
Maud Wagner Teaches Tattooing ... 63
Queen Nanny of the Maroons Teaches Guerilla Warfare ... 64
Josephine Baker Teaches Singing ... 65
Iva Toguri Teaches Patriotism ... 66
Marie-Madeline-Marguerite d'Aubray Teaches Decision Making ... 67
Ranavalona I Teaches Revolution ... 68
Christiana Edmunds Teaches Temperament ... 69
Leonarda Cianciulli Teaches Curse Breaking ... 70
Mary Anning Teaches Fossil Hunting ... 71
Marie Baker Teaches Using Your Assets ... 72
Sarah Good Teaches Spellcasting ... 73
Franceska Mann Teaches Balance ... 74
Olympe de Gouges Teaches Activism ... 75
Annette Kellerman Teaches Marine Biology ... 77
Junko Tabei Teaches Rock Climbing ... 79
Timoclea Teaches Repercussions ... 80

Author Profile ... 81

Anne Boleyn Teaches Patience
Anne Boleyn (1500-1536) was the mistress, turned wife of Henry VIII, and mother of Queen Elizabeth I. In the end, she lost her head for the crime of being unable to produce a male heir.

They will call you witch,
enchantress of men.
I mastered the tongues.
I mothered a monarchy.
Men will destroy religions,
raise new ones from the ashes
all in your name.
I was the original tower girl.
They will try to trap you in that same small room.
Do not let your hair grow long,
cut it off at the neck
like they did to me,
artery bursting, draining onto the floor.
Can they still smell the blood?
Hear my final words echo in their ears?
Am I still soaking their every step?

Elisabeth Bathory Teaches Self Care

Elisabeth Bathory (1560-1614) was countess of Hungary who, when left alone in her castle, decided to dabble in dark magic in order to maintain her young and beautiful looks. She was found guilty of killing over 500 people and lived the rest of her life locked in her bedroom.

They sent me away,
stuck me in a castle and left me there alone.
Don't let them guilt you into growing old and ugly.
Don't listen when they tell you
that the dead are rolling in their graves.
The men who call you "baby",
who ask if your daddy knows where you are.
Trap them in your dungeon.
Slit their throats and bathe in their blood.
Those are the disposable men,
the ones your witchcraft was meant to kill.
Slice them up,
and when they yell,
when they scream at you to stop,
look down at them.
Smile your youthful smile.
Tell them "Baby, if your daddy knew where you were,
he'd roll over in his grave."

Good Advice from Bad Women

Lizzie Borden Teaches How to Get What You Want

Lizzie Borden (1860-1927) was put on trial for the gruesome murder of her father and stepmother in the summer of 1892. She was found not guilty by lack of evidence and lived out her life, mostly alone, never telling the true story
of that horrific day.

Say you are too much rebellion.
Say you are a traumatized girl.
Say you've been too much on your own.
Sad child.
Mad child.
Must be crazy.
Must have lost your damn mind.
No woman can act like that,
so abrasive.
Must have not been loved enough,
just a funny woman;
you are such a funny woman.
Let them believe what they like.
Whatever helps them pray over dinner.
Whatever helps them tuck their babies into bed.
Whatever helps them rest easy at night.
When they question you;
when they point their fingers and sneer in the street,
don't be afraid to burn it all to the ground
and dance on the grave of the ashes.

Madame Alexe Popova Teaches Sisterhood

Madame Alexe Popova (1850s-1909) is known for poisoning perhaps over 300 abusive and horrible men in Russia. She ran a business helping abused women rid themselves of their husband and never gave up the names of her clients or the people on her "staff" who helped commit the crimes.

She tells me in a thick Russian accent,
I am a public servant.
I am the mistress of justice.
When your sister is bleeding on the floor,
when your friend is soaked through,
when her mother hides around corners.
And those men,
how they take and take giving nothing back,
how they think only of the taking.
I say, it was their own fault,
how they drank it down.
I watched them foam at the mouth,
twitch and writhe on the floor.
I saw the beast inside of them slow and die.
Even the strongest men cannot lift their arms under 6 feet of dirt.
Kept the names to myself.
That currency,
the blood and bruises as good as coins and notes.
They will want to pull it from your throat.
Sew your mouth shut, child,
the only pain those men will know now
are the maggots eating out their eyes.
I did good.
You did good.

Ma Barker Teaches Motherhood

Ma Barker (1873-1935) was mother to four unruly and untamable boys; she refused to let their own father discipline them. The boys fell into a life of crime and after losing her eldest son in a police shootout she joined them. She fought hard alongside her boys and died in a shootout herself with her gun still in her hand alongside one of her sons.

You know what they say kid,
family comes first.
How they say blood is thicker than water;
that includes blood spilled.
Your children are all you got,
so, when they send you to the movies,
when they huddle together with plans to make you rich,
fight tooth and nail on their side.
Motherhood begins to smell a lot like blood,
sweat and gunpowder,
and losing a child feels like
carving a piece of your heart out with a dull knife.
So arm yourself,
don't be afraid to die holding your gun in one hand
and your child in the other.

Virginia Hill Teaches Priorities

Virginia Hill (1916-1966) was the well-known mob girlfriend and eventual wife of Bugsy Siegal. She often ran information, or money across borders her lover could not cross and they called her "Flamingo". When Bugsy got nabbed however, she claimed to not know him at all.

She wears a wide brimmed hat,
wrapped in furs;
she waits for me to light her cigarette.
Such a powerful woman,
I think I love her.
She leans forward, and I watch her cherry red lips
when she speaks.
You gotta look out for number one.
Even in love, and especially in money.
They'll trust you with anything,
but when the other shoe drops,
you've never heard of them.
Never even heard the name.
Sit up straight kiddo,
and you smile a thousand watts,
"Accomplice? What kind of word is that?"
Mama always told me,
don't bite the hand that feeds you,
so I made sure it was my hand doing the feeding.

They told me to primp and preen,
"Stand tall, flamingo girl".

In the end though,
it was me sleeping pretty
while they were the ones trapped in cages.

Moll Cutpurse Teaches Confidence

Moll Cutpurse (1584-1659) was a London thief and leader of a gang called Black Dogs. She quickly became famous until King Charles I made it illegal to fence stolen goods. After the King's new laws took effect, Moll retired from gang life though she continued to steal until her death.

If they can't remember your name
carve it into their feet.
So, whenever they think of you,
they'll remember to watch their step.
Look them in the eye while you rob them blind.
Heinous woman.
Villainous.
Bad girl.
Show them what bad girls do.
Watch them kneel before you;
watch them roll your cigarettes
before you've finished the one in your mouth.
They'll pour whiskey down your throat by the gallon.
When they call you "danger",
they really mean "empress".
When they sing God Save the King,
they're singing your name.

Tituba Teaches Acceptance

Tituba (1670s-?) was a south American slave who lived in New England, Salem to be exact. She was accused of witchcraft and after being beaten, confessed to save her life. She was sentenced to jail, but eventually she and the other accused "witches" were pardoned. When she was released, she disappeared and was never heard from again.

They call you witch girl,
call you sorceress,
call you the Devil's child bride
before they call you by your name.
All because I made up a story for children at bedtime,
as all adults make up stories for children at bedtime.
When they call you evil,
do not speak.
When they call you murderess,
point a crooked finger at the blood on their hands.
While you gasp for air around the rope on your neck.
Smile,
and say thank you.
They have no idea the spell that is coming for them.

Good Advice from Bad Women

Rose O'Neal Greenhow Teaches Loyalty
Rose Greenhow (1817-1864) was a spy for the confederacy during the Civil War and would throw lavish parties in order to get information for confederate troops. She drowned when her ship was sunk by the union.

I was the party girl:
saw all of those noses turned up at me,
all those mustaches twisting,
all those false laughs at my girl jokes.
That little debutant,
how I dressed her down
and pinned the note just so between her hair and cap.
Why must men talk and talk and talk,
believing that our silly girl ears are not listening.
I drank in every word,
committed it to memory and passed it along.
Even the Queen loosened her lips for me.
They always trust the woman pouring the champagne.
The water was cold and unforgiving.
It filled my lungs and made my skirts heavy.
It pulled me to the bottom.
But when I looked up I could still see the stars.
From under the current I reminded myself:
loyalty never dies.

Salome Teaches Revenge

Salome (circa 14-71 CE) was stepdaughter to a Roman governor with a big problem. John The Baptist often spoke out against Salome's mother after Salome's father left them for his mistress. Salome began to strip at her stepfather's parties in order to seduce them into getting what she wanted. In this case, what she wanted was John the Baptist's head.

A girl is capable of anything to honor her mother,
even from a man of God,
who slaughters his sheep while they lay in the field.
I could smell his blood in my dreams.
I fantasized about the sound of his screams.
Men in power will do anything to get what they want,
and, oh, how they wanted me.
They begged for the music to begin.
They pleaded for me to enter a room.
They would have prayed to my silks if I told them to.
Instead, I demanded justice,
and they brought me his head.
The stares I got,
walking through town, holding him by the hair.
The smile on my mother's face,
when she stared into his empty eyes.
They were the same stares I got when I dropped my silks.
Let them stare, I think,
because when they finally blink, they'll realize,
they've been eating out of my hand the whole damn time.

Anne Bonney and Mary Read Teach Friendship

Anne Bonney and Mary Read (late 1600s-1720s) were female pirates and best friends who were captured with their ship defending it against 45 men while the rest of the crew and captain were below deck drinking and playing cards. Both women were pardoned on the grounds of them both being pregnant at the time of the trial.

Anne clears her throat,
Please excuse this mouthy girl,
her hive full of wasp's throat,
her rows and rows of shark's teeth.
Being broke on the high seas is still richer than any king.
Tell me I can't and watch me succeed.
Mary clears her throat,
I'd rather smell of gunpowder than perfume anyway.
I built mountains on waves.
Listen when I say,
if a man touches you without your permission,
challenge him to a duel,
make sure you shoot first.
Together they smirk,
Us girls gotta stick together even when dressed as men,
and two against 45 isn't fair for any gender.
The only favor our womanhood ever granted
was in the end.
Fight like a man or hang like a dog,
good thing we fight like girls.
And their glasses clink and it sounds like heaven.

Mary Tudor Teaches Conviction

Mary "Bloody Mary" Tudor (1516-1558) was daughter from Henry VIII's first marriage, who was disowned and then found her way back onto the throne and set out to make England catholic instead of protestant. She murdered many protestants which earned her the nickname.

They will cower;
they will whisper at the sound of your heavy skirts.
You, sweet, hideous, forest fire of a woman.
You, bastard child of the monarchy.
You, banished beauty.
Hide under the floorboards,
your crosses,
your bibles,
the very center of yourself.
Take your time,
wait your turn,
make your move.
Ride in and take the head off the Devil yourself.
They will look at you walking away and call you snake.
Hiss when they pass you,
because there is one thing they cannot call you:
weak.

Calamity Jane Teaches Storytelling

Calamity Jane (1852-1903) was a solider, Indian killer and eventually joined Buffalo Bill's Wild West Show. She caused chaos wherever she went and often told tall tales about her life that never truly added up.

Take caution of the whirlwind girl,
take shelter from her womanly storm.
Let them stare in awe of the damage.
I was the knight in shining armor,
I was prince charming.
Swig whiskey,
smoke cigars,
sharpshooter,
reckless girl.
The difference between lies and stories
is what gets written down.
Always keep 'em guessing.

Peggy Shippen Arnold Teaches Staying Humble

Peggy Shippen Arnold (1760-1804) was wife to Benedict Arnold who was a British spy during the revolution and eventually roped her husband into betraying the American side as well.

I was the mastermind.
I was the planner.
I planted the seeds.
I watered the soil.
Spy girl,
scheming, sneaking, snake of a woman.
Faint at the sight of blood,
delicate lady,
sweet girl,
so pretty;
just a pretty little girl.
History may not remember but I sure as hell will.
How they echo the names of men,
all of their accomplishments stolen from women.
My husband's name became synonymous with betrayal,
but mine,
they worshiped it.
I was their hero.
Don't let one side of history be the only one getting told.
You are a goddamn hero.

Catherine the Great Teaches the Value of a Good Education

Catherine The Great (1729-1796) was a German princess determined to be a Queen. She studied languages, history and politics after marrying the future tsar of Russia. When her husband was "mysteriously" killed as well as two other contenders for the throne, Catherine finally got her place in power.

Girls just want to have fun,
and funds,
and pure, unadulterated power.
When the weak men run,
when they scuffle away like rats to the sewers,
make your move.
I had the people.
I had the power,
and they loved it.
They needed me.
I made them special, and they thanked me for it.
Smart queen,
witty queen,
brilliant queen,
savvy queen,
clever queen,
our queen.
Stick to your plan girl.
They will chant for you,
as they did for me,
and you will be great.

Belle Starr Teaches Confidence

Belle Starr (1848-1889) was a confederate spy during the Civil War who eventually married a Cherokee man, Sam Starr. She thieved, sold bootleg liquor, and could talk her way out of any spot of trouble. She is rumored to have been killed by one of her ex-boyfriends, husbands or sons.

Lanky,
bony,
awkward girl.
Looks more like a boy, girl.
Mean mouth girl.
Face like a blade,
larger than life,
storybook girl.
Didn't stop me from charming money into my pocket.
Didn't stop me from charming men to my bed.
Didn't stop me from charming the police at my door.
Girl just likes a bad boy.
Girl just likes a clean boy,
a boy she can rough up,
a bit of dirt under the fingernails,
ash in the lungs,
bullet between the ears.
They'll fear you.
They'll quiver at the sound of your steps.
They'll be scared shitless of you.
They'll have to shoot you in the back,
because one look at you,
they'll think "sorry" was their name.

Pearl Hart Teaches Personal Freedom

Pearl Hart (1871-1925) grew up obsessed with the south and after leaving her abusive husband she moved to Arizona and robbed a stagecoach. She became an Arizonan sensation being the only woman to have ever committed a robbery of this kind and was eventually pardoned for refusing to be tried by laws written by men.

Mama taught me to be a good girl,
nice girl,
lips shut tight girl.
So the first time he raised a hand to me,
when he hunted me down like a dog,
should've stuck a bullet in him.
Only had to up and enlist to get away,
still wasn't far enough.
Went all the way to the Grand Canyon,
shouted into the vastness of it,
turned on my heel and brought the desert to its knees.
Won't live by the laws of men,
the ones who hit me,
who called me "kiddo",
who find me no better than the dust on their boots.
Good girl,
nice girl,
but no more
lips shut tight girl.

Jezebel Teaches Religion

Jezebel (9th century BC) was a queen hated for her choice of Gods to worship. She was eventually thrown out of power, trampled by civilians, and eaten by dogs.

I was the bad girl,
naughty party princess,
deplorable queen.
It's my name that echoes around the world,
because I chose to worship my gods.
Was I the only one building altars?
The only one praying for peace?
No,
but I was the woman
and I was talking
which is equivalent to guilt.
So, I dressed in the finest silk,
I lined my eyes in black.
When they trampled me in the street,
I felt their every step.
When the dogs pulled at my skin with their teeth,
I prayed to my gods.
They held me to their chests,
kissed my head,
and said "Child,
welcome home"

Delilah Teaches Being Truthful
Delilah (110 BCE) is best known for finding Samson's weakness, his hair, and exploiting it. However, when Samson gained back his strength while being kept as Delilah's prisoner and destroyed the city, Delilah was long gone.

Those men,
those men who lie,
how they tell us what they think we want to hear.
How they cover their ears to our protests.
How when we outwit them,
they call it luck.
Lie again to me boy.
I'm keeping count.
I'll find your weakness
and exploit it.
I may be the villain,
the world's original mean girl,
the universe's caution tale,
but only one of us sinned.
I can't wait to watch you squirm your way out of this one.

Beulah Annan and Belva Gaertner Teach
The Price of Fame

Beulah (circa 1901-1928) was the inspiration for Roxie Hart in the play and film Chicago; she famously killed her lover and tricked her husband into using all of his money to hire successful mob lawyer William O'Brian. She was set free and divorced her husband. Belva Gaertner was the inspiration for Velma Kelly, who allegedly killed her husband and his mistress though she claimed to remember none of it. They were known as the Merry Murderesses in the papers; she was set free as well.

Beulah begins,
firecracker girl,
slams a hand down hard.
They called me crazy,
called it a jealous rage,
called it self-defense.
Sing a song,
do a dance,
forget my damn name.
when I was the one in the paper,
I was the one doing all the work.
The next time they call me Roxie,
I'll remind 'em "merry murderess"
isn't all song and dance.
Belva who has waited her turn,
puts a hand on Beulah's shoulder and smiles.
They got part of it right.
I didn't remember,
or at least I said I didn't.
But they forget I started that saying,
about the fish in the sea,
about how no man could be worth being kept in a cage.
So when you think of me,
don't think of Velma,
the black bob,
the fringe dress,
remember this:
he isn't worth it.

Cleopatra Teaches Politics

Cleopatra (69 B.C-30 B.C) was ruler of the Ptolemaic Kingdom of Egypt. She was also a diplomat, naval commander, linguist and medical author. Throughout her lifetime she charmed many powerful men with her distinct beauty and even defeated her own brother for the throne.

Power hungry bitch.
Too much eyeliner bitch.
Talks too much bitch.
Laughs too loud bitch.
Underestimated bitch.
Kills her own brother bitch.
Just wants a seat at the table bitch.
If they say you shouldn't have something,
step on their neck while you take it.
If you can't have Egypt,
take Rome.
Power is power wherever it's held.
Those selfish boys,
watch them drown in their own shiny things.
You, clever girl,
how you make them love you,
pull them into your web and feast on them.
And in the end,
when you return home
to the ones who scorned you
do not hold a grudge.
Do not be unkind.
Sit on your throne.
Do not give up your power,
keep it clutched in your fist.
Give it only to the earth,
let Mother bleed you dry.
Die like a queen.

Bonnie Parker Teaches True Love

*Bonnie Parker (1910-1934) is most famously known as part of the Barrow Gang. Girlfriend of Clyde Barrow; the couple tragically were stopped by police and died together in a gruesome shootout with the cops. Bonnie was often published in newspapers sending in poems including one in which she predicts
her and Clyde's deaths.*

Ravishing redhead,
rebel rouser,
rifle wielding,
robber girl.
They fell in love with me.
Papers worshipped me,
police dreamt of catching me,
men dreamt of having me.
But for me,
there was only ever him,
my Clyde.
He hated the other man's name tattooed on my hip,
but we wear the scars we choose,
and all of my scars,
the bullets, the scrapes,
every scabbed knee or elbow,
echoed his name on my body.
He'd steal the moon if I asked him to,
and I would have given anything for us
to stay just the way we were,
when it was just him and me
watching rain on the windowpane.
Or his smile when he drove a fast car,
or his laugh when I told a joke.
I knew it couldn't last,
even wrote it down on paper.
Didn't mind dying as long as it was next to him,
and in the end it was.
See kid, the dying part was easy,
the laying my head down on his chest,

the bullet holes like the top of a saltshaker.

The hard part was loving him.
There was too much love
and not enough of me to hold it.
Sometimes,
I loved him like a bank robbery,
fast and angry and yelling and violent.
Sometimes,
I loved him like a V8 engine,
mechanical and rhythmic,
like it was what my body was built to do.
But sometimes,
sometimes,
I loved him like a photograph,
frozen and still and smiling.
That was my favorite way to love,
frozen, still, and smiling.
The kind of love that you hang on a wall.
The kind of love you want to frame in a museum.
The kind of love that lasts forever.

Good Advice from Bad Women

Mata Hari Teaches the Power of Sexuality

Mata Hari (1876-1917) was a professional dancer and mistress who, in her later years, became a French spy during WWI. When she started to seduce a German captain, she was branded a spy and was killed by firing squad.

When I danced,
rooms fell silent.
When I danced,
my mind fell silent.
Like loving a man,
this rhythm I found so easily;
the music made from my hips.
They shot me in the street,
like a dog.
They called me spy,
called me dirty,
called me devil.
But I was always on the right side.
Defending my home,
my people,
my men,
whom I loved.
For women,
when the dancing days are behind us,
our hips can only do us so many favors.
But our lips,
our lips can crumble countries.
They took me to the street,
they called me spy,
called me dirty,
called me devil,
but they never called me ugly.
Never called me old.
Never called me hag.
Because even as they press
the hollow lip of a gun to my temple,
They are thinking of my hips.

Mary Mallon Teaches Passion

Mary Mallon (1869-1938) also known as Typhoid Mary was an Irish immigrant who worked as a cook in many homes. She was found out to be the only healthy carrier of typhoid virus and infected 51 people. Mary however, felt she was wrongly accused and ran from the police, when they caught her, finally, they kept her in isolation at North Border Hospital. Along with the stool samples the government tested (most of them coming back positive) Mary sent samples to a different lab and they all came back negative. Mary eventually died in isolation.

I was told as a child
sick is seen.
Sick girls do not run in the fields,
sick girls do not laugh and play,
sick girls cannot cook peaches and cream.
But the soft skin of the peaches never decayed in my hands,
the cream never turned sour as I gently folded it.
What do these people know of me?
Try to tell me I'm ill,
call my blood poison,
say my body is killing people without my permission.
Of course I ran,
when American men bang at your door,
when they threaten to lock you in a cage,
never to smell the sweet scent of heavy cream,
never to feel the juice of a peach dribble down your chin,
never to see the smile on the face of someone tasting your heart.
They locked me up,
stole my insides,
called me poison.
But I know what I was,
different.
Sounds different,
looks different,
swears different.
Must be poison,
to this country,

this land of the free,
that locked me in a cage,
and called me poison.
In the end,
I died in that room.
I rest in a tomb labeled
"Poison Woman".
But in heaven there are no stone rooms,
there are no American men,
with heavy hands
that touch without asking.
There are only ripe peaches,
And sweet cream.

Eve Teaches Blame

Eve, better known as the first wife, was made from Adam's rib and lived in the Garden of Eden with her husband. The bible story tells that God gave them freedom in the garden, but they were not to eat from one specific tree. Seduced by the tree and encouraged by a snake (Satan), Eve eats an apple from the tree, committing the first sin. She encourages Adam to also eat from the apple and the two are banished from the garden cursing them and all of their offspring to a life of sinning.

That bitch.
That apple eating bitch.
That can't follow directions bitch.
Her fault, it was all her fault,
can't keep her hands to herself.
And Adam,
Adam who put himself on the line.
Adam who gave up his own body for her.
What a selfish woman.
Or, what a naïve man,
taking a bite as well.
What a lonely man.
Willing to rip himself apart for someone to talk to,
to hold his fragile body,
to give him permission to want.
When a man and a woman
commit the same crime,
the woman must be at fault.
That evil seductress
who enchanted him into sin.
Where is Adam's place?
Where is God's?
Who gave them a garden with freedom to roam,
but one tree that would damn them.
Damn their children, and their children's children.
When will we stop carrying the crimes of our ancestors?
When will it stop weighing on us,
soaking our skin, like acid rain,
burning through everything in its path.

Joan of Arc Teaches Sainthood

Joan of Arc (1412-1431) was nicknamed the Maid of Orleans for her part in the Hundred Years War. Joan claimed to have heard the voices of saints in her head telling her how to end the war and help Charles VII be crowned rightful king of France. She was captured in battle and burned at the stake for witchcraft.
King Charles VII, who'd often ask Joan for advice from her Saints, denied any connection to her and Joan died on the pyre.
She was later granted Sainthood nearly 500 years after her death.

Just a farmgirl, such a simple mind,
and this is who God speaks through,
of all the priests and popes,
of every man in Rome,
this silly, simple girl?
Yes. Why wouldn't God choose her?
A woman, someone able to command bodies.
They whispered, snickered behind their armor.
They called her witch girl, demon,
even the crown, who had begged for her,
who had armor fitted to her girl body.
Even he turned around,
pretended he could not hear the screams.
How they pressed the knife to her throat,
signed that gift away in blood,
and still she burned.
But as she burned she did not cry,
did not let the stench of charred flesh fill her nose.
She breathed. She prayed.
And now they call her 'saint',
how they praise her name,
how they beg her forgiveness,
and she gives it, freely.
Because she knows what we all know.
In a time of war,
they followed her,
and won.
How is that not Godly?

Lady Godiva Teaches Body Positivity

Godiva, Countess of Mercia (990 AD-1067) is best known for riding naked through the streets of Coventry covered only by her golden hair. How that truly happened goes like this: her husband Leofric, was taxing the people so harshly they could hardly afford food for their families. Godiva begged her husband to lessen the taxes many times and eventually, he agreed but only if Godiva would ride through town completely naked (a real shock in that time). Godiva took one for the team and rode through Coventry covered only in her long hair and her husband had no choice but to see his side of the bet through.

I was the bull.
And him with greedy hands,
the matador.
Steam from my nose,
drool from my mouth,
dare me
I snarl.
And with a swing of his red cape,
and the jingle of coins in his pocket,
he dared me.
Give up your body,
the only thing you truly own,
bare your skin,
save them with your curves.
And like the bull,
I charged.
Nothing but my hair.
For my country,
for my people,
for men like him,
to stop taking whatever they like,
whenever they like it.

Emily Hobhouse Teaches Feminism

Emily Hobhouse (1860-1926) is best known as an advocate for British Welfare. She traveled to South Africa and found that the concentration camps built there by the British were in deplorable conditions. She brought this to the attention of the British people and the outrage sparked the government to reconsider the conditions. She was eventually deported from Britain for her investigations but returned to dedicate herself to the education of women.

Angel of love,
educator of women,
un-patriot,
disagreeable lady.
Should have stayed in that house,
with all of my bibles
and prayers
and counting the stones of each wall,
over,
and over.
Us girls,
who read,
who raise our hands in class,
who shout and scream
at your atrocities.
They sent me away.
As if throwing a stone further down the stream
doesn't also make ripples.
Gag my mouth shut,
rip these books from my hands,
you cannot have my mind.
Cannot take what I know.
I am not enamored by your smooth voice.
I do not swoon at your sweet words.
I care only about your injustices,
and the destruction of them.

Amelia Earhart Teaches Fearlessness

Amelia Earhart (1897-1939) was not declared dead until two years after her disappearance over the Pacific Ocean in 1937. She is most well known for being the first female aviator to fly solo across the Atlantic Ocean. She disappeared on her Pacific flight and was never heard from again although there are many conspiracies about what happened to her.

Flight girl,
always on the run,
from everything,
or perhaps,
toward something else.
They will tell you no,
say you can't,
say you shouldn't.
That your frail woman body cannot handle,
the height of your dreams.
They're wrong.
Take it from me,
you are not only the bird,
but the wind pushing it forward.
Not only the wave,
but the moon controlling the tides.
You are not just the rain on the roof,
you are the whole damn storm.

Sylvia Pankhurst Teaches Forgiveness

Sylvia Pankhurst (1882-1960) was a prominent campaigner of the suffragette movement in England. Her letters were used as the basis for an article exposing the horrible treatment of suffragettes in jails and led to many changes in prison policies as well as greatly helping the suffragette movement overall.

They censored the history books,
didn't talk about what it must have felt like,
how your teeth became weak and weak and weaker,
until falling out of your skull.
Or how the taste of blood was like pennies on your tongue.
How the screams came morning and night,
and even when you were too tired to fight,
your body knew it was wrong.
They forget the word strike,
also means choice when they make you thank them
on your way out.
You, with your soft heart,
noting how they were victims too.
You, with that forgiveness,
so many still have not mastered.
They censored the history books,
perhaps for fear of its repetition,
but it happened on its own,
in the cyclical way it always would.
The only difference is,
animals grow to evolve,
and our teeth are much stronger today.
But that doesn't mean we can forget,
does not offer any sense of safety.
They censored the history books,
so, we began shouting your names from rooftops,
whispering them in corridors,
passing them in notes to strangers walking by.
Let them try to stamp this out.
Let them try to censor us away now.

Boudica Teaches Retribution

Boudica (30-61 A.D) was queen of British Celtic Inceni tribe who led an uprising against the Roman Empire. The Romans who invaded her tribe, killing many and even imprisoning and raping Boudica's children were not defeated which led to Boudica supposedly killing herself.

It was called a blood rampage.
They named me savage.
They called me animal.
80,000.
I could have bathed in the blood.
160,000 unblinking eyes.
I call it revenge,
my pound of flesh.
They asked me why,
on bent knee,
tear-stained cheeks,
begging around the blood filling their mouths.
They asked me how.
How a woman,
a mother,
could be so thirsty.
To them I said,
even a lioness,
will rip out your throat,
when you threaten her cubs.

Mary Shelley Teaches Inspiration

Mary Shelley (1797-1851) is best known as the mother of the science fiction genre. She was married to Percy Shelley in 1816 and was often surrounded by prominent writers of the time who would advise each other on their writing. She also edited the works of her husband, and wrote many other works, none however as famous as the gothic novel, Frankenstein.

Like dirt and blood,
the things I made were never meant to mix.
I was only ever meant to sit,
watch the greatness,
exploit myself for a man,
who so often wanted silence from me.
My husband,
his heart,
a stone on my desk,
beating in my chest,
breathing into me a dream.
Who could write something like this?
So manic,
This thing that reaches out
with cold dead hands,
grasping for something.
They liked me better,
when I was anonymous.
But I liked me better,
as I was.
Loud.
Taking up space,
with my cold, dead, hands.

Marie Antoinette Teaches Apology

Marie Antoinette (1755-1793) was the last Queen of France before the French Revolution. She is best known for saying "let them eat cake" in response to the starving people of France. However, there is never any historical evidence of her saying anything of the sort and she is often depicted as a quiet and withdrawn girl who often took the tragedies of the French people very close to heart. She let herself be blamed by the French people for spending all of the country's money on "frivolous" whims of a teenage queen.

Teenage queen,
at the line between child and woman,
they stripped me
of everything
even the clothes on my back.
Didn't matter if I wanted it.
Teenage queen,
when you are given the world,
possibilities are endless.
And hatred is like,
jewels around the neck;
the sparkle is intoxicating.
Didn't matter if it was real.
Teenage queen,
I let them hate me,
let them take everything.
When I had nothing left,
they took my head
and with my final breath,
I said what all teenage queens
are taught to say:
I'm sorry;
Didn't matter if I meant it.

Artemisia Gentileschi Teaches Art Appreciation

Artemisia Gentileschi (1593-1653) was an Italian Baroque painter and is considered one of the most accomplished painters of her time. She often depicted women from mythology or bible stories in positions of power and her work especially blossomed after winning a very publicized rape trial against her teacher. The trial eventually ruined her reputation, but fueled her art leading to her post-mortem fame.

The men who teach you,
who tell you you're brilliant,
who believe in you the most.
Those men will also,
pluck you from your roots,
tear each petal from your fragile stem,
crush you in their hands,
hang you to dry.
They will return,
again,
and again,
call it a lesson.
Tell you you're learning.
Your revenge,
will be sweet,
a stroke of paint on canvas,
a story of murder,
in your medium.
Their name,
paint over it in inky black,
bloom a new story over the stain.
You are every warrior,
every success,
every failure,
in every color spectrum.

Ching Shih Teaches Achievement

Ching Shih (1775-1844) was a prostitute turned wife of Cheng I, a former pirate. Part of her agreement to marry the pirate was that she receive a prominent place of power on the ship. She also advocated for marriage rights for other women brought aboard, such as monogamous relationships. She rose in power and eventually gained amnesty for herself and all pirates from the government.

What a woman.
Woman who dreams,
woman who achieves,
woman who leaves.
They never expected it.
Never expect that something they own,
would up and walk away,
slice them apart as you leave.
Join the boys,
teach them how to live pretty,
how to run graceful,
how to steal gorgeous.
Watch them bloom beneath your loving hand.
In the distance,
enemy flags approach.
Remain as calm as the tide during the dry season.
They will never catch you,
no one will ever own you again.

Abigail Adams Teaches Democracy

Abigail Adams (1744-1818) is best known as wife and closest advisor of second U.S. President, John Adams as well as mother of John Quincy Adams, sixth U.S. President. Abigail was abhorred by men of the time who believed she had no place in American democracy, especially as advisor to the President. Abigail however, seemed to pay them no attention and continued advising her husband.

Arrogant girl,
domineering child,
outspoken lady.
Girl reading,
girl writing,
girl speaking.
Why is it the same as opening fire in a crowd?
Why do they point fingers?
Why do they stare in awe,
mouth gaping like some bottom feeder,
skimming garbage off of the sea floor.
Why does standing for something
mean I must be destroying something else in its place?
Isn't this all just free speech?
Isn't all this what we built this country on?
Do you only fear it when it is wearing a skirt?
Shake in your boots,
tremble at the stroke of this ink.
This girly page,
which you imagine smells of my perfume.
I was taught by the same scholars.
I read the same books.
And what I learned is this:
speak up or die quiet.

Grace O'Malley Teaches Confident Mindset

Grace O'Malley (1530-1603) was lord of the O Maille dynasty in the west of Ireland and a well-known pirate queen. She is best known for refusing to give in to Elizabeth I, and at one point during a meeting with the Queen even refusing to bow because she considered herself Elizabeth's equal. To save herself and her crew however, she became a military advisor to Elizabeth I, eventually gaining the Queen's respect and friendship.

If they try to tell you
that you are not worthy,
spill your own blood.
Let them see it not run red,
but as gold as heaven itself.
They will try to take advantage,
at a time they believe you are weakest.
Appear.
Bloodied,
arms raised,
screaming,
bring hell upon them.
I was a queen,
who did not need a crown.
I was the heir to an empire,
I held men's lives in my hands.
I do not bow,
I do not lower myself.
And neither do you;
not anymore.

Florence Nightingale Teaches Cleanliness
Florence Nightingale (1820-1910) is best known as serving as manager and trainer of nurses during the Crimean war. When Nightingale arrived at the battlefield she was disgusted by the poor facilities and care wounded soldiers were receiving and eventually changed the care tactics, changing the face of medicine at the time.

I was never meant to be there.
Never meant to see them,
lying in their own filth,
bathing in dirty water.
They tried to shield me from it.
Wanted to keep me pristine,
fresh out of the box,
still smelling of tissue paper.
Those men,
those boys,
just children,
still looking at the world with new eyes.
Trying to be brave.
We covered them in mud,
and blood,
and bile.
We called it heroism;
I did not.
I lived in a pristine place.
I saw the world the way it should be;
a breath of fresh spring air,
and remade it in my image.
So when you see the world as it is,
the dirt of it,
the grime,
the mess of it all,
pull your sleeves up,
and wipe it clean.

Marie Curie Teaches Anatomy of a Superhero
Marie Curie (1867-1934) is best known for her work with spouse Pierre Curie and discovering two elements, radium and polonium. Her greatest invention was the Petit Curie, a portable x ray machine that would save lives in many wars. She is also known for being the first woman to win not one, but two Nobel prizes.

The world's first radiation-soaked genius.
Evil,
is everywhere.
Molecular,
smaller than the space between breaths,
bigger than the dead air between stars.
Forget those men,
the ones who stop listening as soon as you speak,
who don't believe what you say,
unless it is repeated by a man.
They will regret this,
dismissing you.
They will wish they were bathed in your discovery.
They will want to be poisoned,
like you.
Those others,
the men who fight crime in picture books,
they have nothing on our superpowers.

Clementine Delait Teaches Certainty

Clementine Delait (1865-1939) is known as the original bearded lady. She and her husband kept a café in France where Clementine was often asked to pose for photographs or sign autographs. Her fame skyrocketed when she visited a carnival and seeing the bearded woman attraction was appalled and boasted that she could grow a better beard herself. Her confidence and facial hair made her so famous that many people even began trading her photographs like baseball cards.

She looks at me,
strokes her gorgeous, hairy chin,
and when she laughs,
it infects the air with a joy I've never known.
Aren't I beautiful?
And aren't you?
And aren't we all?
You are used to hiding,
I can tell by the way you walk,
I can hear it when you speak.
I remember how it felt,
heart like an anvil,
hands full of razor blades,
tongue like the desert.
You,
are lightning.
You,
a tsunami child.
Would you ever ask the sun to dim its shine?
For the moon to stop pulling the ocean?
Stop expecting your body to riot against its nature.
Let yourself grow,
let them gawk and stare,
let them wish they could have what you've got.
And when you die,
do not let them speak for you.
Girls like us,
write our own elegies.

Lucille Ball Teaches Bossiness

Lucille Ball (1911-1989) is best known as the star of sitcoms such as I Love Lucy and The Lucy Show. She was also a studio executive and producer of her own shows. She is often regarded as harsh, bossy and rude by people she "feuded" with; however, many describe her as stubborn, strong willed and a great leader. She changed the face of not only Hollywood but women's places in it.

When I walked into the room,
people sat up straighter.
When I spoke,
people leaned in close.
Not because of my hair,
not because of my dress,
but because of what I had to say.
It was important,
not to them,
but to me,
and they could tell.
When I left the room,
people slouched,
they crinkled their noses,
they spat the poisonous saliva out of their mouths.
They called me bitch.
Because of my hair,
because of my dress,
despite what I'd had to say.
I want to remind them of,
Elizabeth I,
Queen Victoria,
the Virgin Mary.
Of those women before me;
who walked into rooms
where they were unwelcome,
who spoke
when they were told to be quiet.
How those women changed the whole world.
So why couldn't I?

Hedy Lamarr Teaches Being Too Much

Hedy Lamarr (1914-2000) is best known as the most beautiful actress in Hollywood as well as performing the first ever female orgasm shown in film. However, Hedy was also a prolific scientist and invented frequency hopping which led to the invention of GPS, Bluetooth and WIFI.

Ask a question.
Mirror, mirror on the wall,
who is the fairest?
Who is the brainiest?
Who is the bravest?
Who is the sex object-est?
Who is the taking up the most space-est?
It is you.
They won't like it.
Note, how it makes them uncomfortable.
Jot down your hypothesis,
of how they are afraid of a woman who is too much.
Who talks too much.
Who laughs too much.
Who lines her lips with the shade of red they hate-too much.
Who speaks without being spoken to-too much.
Who teaches them too much.
A woman like you.
Publish your findings,
in every journal,
in every paper,
on every cocktail napkin.
Watch your discovery grow,
watch it impact everything.
Watch the "too much" of you,
overtake them, like vines of ivy,
running uncut through the trellis,
during the rainy season.
Turn back to the mirror,
ask it:
what next?

Lozen Teaches the Art of War

Lozen (1840-1889) is best known as an Apache chief and many believed she was a prophet, given powers to sense the direction in which the enemy would invade. She was also a sharpshooter and gifted with horses. She was a trusted ally of Geronimo and won many battles for her people.

I walked into the mountains,
I prayed,
returned with a power
thieving white men kill for.
Trained in killing,
but also healing,
and also fighting.
Watch me,
on my horse,
rifle in hand.
Save their lives,
feed the children,
kill the enemy.
All as a woman,
all in my own dark skin.
Hunt our heads,
offer a prize,
for our final breaths.
Because it makes you feel big,
and strong,
and powerful.
But, mark my words,
we were here before you,
we will be here after.
I will inherit the Earth,
and you will merely rot in it.

Nellie Bly Teaches Investigative Journalism

Nellie Bly (1864-1922) is best known for investigating and exposing the poor conditions of mental health institutions in America. This determined woman was outspoken and also broke records, traveling around the world in 72 days. She paved the way for female journalists to take on more challenging and serious stories.

Lonely orphan girl,
poison pen poised,
won't take no for an answer.
Undercover,
disguised girl,
hidden face girl,
don't hide your face girl.
Watch them,
witness their atrocities,
how they locked us up,
our poor souls
guilty of nothing but existing in our own skin.
Hold up your mirror to their grimy faces,
the precious things they claim to own.
Show them the world,
then teach them how to live in it,
properly.

Good Advice from Bad Women

Bettie Page Teaches Single Girl Lifestyle
Bettie Page (1923-2008) was an American pin up model best recognized for her jet-black hair, blue eyes and trademark fringe. She was also an advocate for women's body positivity, sex positivity and single girl lifestyle. She was adored by women and men alike and referred to as the Dark Angel.

SLUT.
Single,
living
under
tyranny.
They called me angel,
dark angel,
only an angel with the lights off,
only an angel when you're all alone,
only an angel in a habit.
Well, I say different.
Angel, lights on.
Angel, crowded room.
Angel, tiny dress.
Angel, on your newsstand.
Angel, on your billboards.
Angel, in every one of your dreams.
When a man told me how to style my hair,
I cut my bangs in the shape of a U.
As in fuck you,
to anyone who thinks they have any say in what I am.
What I wear,
what I say,
what I think.
Poor girl,
they must have said,
whispered to their husbands before bed,
she'll never get a man like that.
But to my face,
in the street,
on the subway,

Good Advice from Bad Women

they begged for advice.

How can you do that?
How can you look in the mirror
and fall in love every morning?
How can I do that?
I tell them,
it's easy.
Listen to the sound of your steps.
Listen to the thwacking of your heels on the concrete,
realize the storm inside of you.
Look at your body,
say thank you.
Quit living like an apology.

Irena Sendler Teaches How to Swim

Irena Sendler (1910-2008) rescued over 2,500 children from concentration camps during the second world war. She had a trained dog who would bark to cover any sound the children would make. She gave them new Christian names and families to live with and kept their given names in jars buried in her yard. At the end of the war she reunited as many children as she could to their families.

Papa always told me,
don't let them drown alone,
when you know how to swim.
Their names,
how I licked the jam jars clean,
shoved their given names inside and buried it.
The Earth never forgets,
so neither would I.
When I handed them the dust covered glass,
their lives from before shoved inside,
they looked at me,
said thank you.
But truly, I should have been thanking them,
those angels, clothed in death,
how badly I wanted to knit them all sweaters,
yarn of love,
light, kindness.
All of the things the world forgot to show them.
I couldn't let them become one of those things.
Those beautiful dead things we talk about
without truly knowing what they were,
like flowers plucked from a sidewalk crack,
plucked and given meaning they didn't ask for.
They deserved a chance to decide their own meaning,
revenge,
forgiveness,
serenity,
it wasn't for me to say.
But only to give them a chance to say for themselves.

Christine Jorgensen Teaches Rolling with The Punches

Christine Jorgensen (1926-1989) was an American actress and entertainer and also the first publicly known American trans women. After going through transitional surgery and hormone therapy she was outed by the New York Daily News who published her private letters. She sold the rights to her story in American Weekly magazine and rode the wave of her fame all the way to the bank.

My letters,
this privacy I was promised,
only in the right body.
Must have been wrong,
wrong kind of woman,
wrong kind of feminine.
Here's my secret,
there is no wrong kind of money.
You want a chance to gawk,
to stare,
to watch the woman at work.
Open your wallet,
hand all of those bills,
covered in those men,
to me.
Their worst nightmare,
because I saw the closed door of their minds,
shoved my foot in the cracks,
pried it open with my bare hands,
and now they see.
Read it in the paper,
watch it on stage,
but please silence your bias,
until the show is over.

Lilith Teaches Demonology

*Lilith was Adam's lesser-known, first wife,
who refused to lie beneath him and left the Garden of Eden.
She is represented as a demon but was omitted from the bible altogether.*

Omit me from your book,
those holy pages.
Paint me in sludge,
drag me through the mud,
through the crust of the Earth.
Call me Queen of Hellfire,
and for what?
For wanting a place at the table,
to speak without being spoken to,
to eat not only crumbs but the whole damn meal.
Who are you?
A man?
Who has decided he is above me?
Woman.
Life giver.
Blooming garden of stars,
split me open and out spills,
seeds.
In the end,
man will not inherit the Earth.
But beast,
beasts such as me,
clawing our way through the blood,
scar,
sweat,
beasts who will crush your table,
burn your garden to the ground,
who will eat everything.
Who will pick you from between their teeth,
muzzle bloodied,
we will be glorious.

Khutulun Teaches Physical Education

Khutulun (1260-1306) was great, great, granddaughter to Genghis Khan and would challenge her suitors to a wrestling match for her hand. She was undefeated for years and eventually married by choice. Many believed she was blessed by the heavens and was chosen over her 14 older brothers to be her father's successor to the throne.

Fight me.
No, really, fight me,
prove you are more than words.
Action, show me,
you want my hand,
and not my crown.
If you should win,
we will rule together,
but if I should win,
if my independence should conquer
your desire to own me,
you will leave.
Disgraced.
Undefeated,
reigning champion of her own hand.
She grins widely,
and something in her smile
makes me want to lift my hands, as well,
to fight for her,
this remarkable woman.
They swore, prayed to their Gods,
that I was blessed by the heavens.
Perhaps I was,
chosen over 14 brothers,
that crown was always mine,
as my body was, as my heart,
until I was ready to give it away.
Hold, girl,
hold onto whatever you have,
don't let them tell you when to let go,
lest you fall to your death.

Elizabeth I Teaches How to Be Alone
Elizabeth I (1533-1603) was the first Queen to rule alone.
She never married, was hot tempered and famously intelligent.
She made England a leader in world power and her time on the throne
is often regarded as the golden age of England.

We have been ruling for centuries.
Appointed by God himself,
why should I share my divinity with a man?
First to my name,
virgin queen,
pure as winter snow,
unafraid to spill blood on the frozen earth,
on this white dress.
Everything I touched turned to power,
bloomed under my supervision,
art,
science,
religion itself,
kneeled to me.
They begged for me,
woman of fire,
rules with iron fist,
a smile and a blade,
a kiss laced in poison,
how something so beautiful,
so enticing,
so demure,
will cut you in half.

Lela Lombardi Teaches Driving Lessons
Lela Lombardi (1941-1992) was the first woman to drive in a Formula One race. The Italian driver learned her love for racing while helping her father deliver meat in his delivery truck. She still holds records in Formula One history that have yet to be beat. She is considered to be the best female driver in racing history.

Fastest woman alive,
faster than all the boys.
First gear,
driving dad's truck,
stop signs blur past.
Second gear,
walk onto the steaming tar road,
striped and arching in an oval,
swing your girl hips as the boys stare,
let the smell of burning rubber fill their noses,
wear that checkered flag like body armor.
Third gear,
let them ask, a girl? A girl?
Is that even allowed?
She can't possibly race,
what about her breasts?
What about her long eyelashes?
What about her estrogen?
Fourth gear,
she must be cheating,
must be her small girl body,
must make her lighter in the car,
more aerodynamic, cheater girl.
Fifth gear,
unbreakable records,
not just the fastest woman,
fastest person, fastest ever.
They can try, let them slip into lead lined shoes,
hold the gas pedal, cut all the brake lines,
they can't beat you,
they don't have what you got.

Maud Wagner Teaches Tattooing

Maud Wagner (1877-1961) is the world's first recorded female tattoo artist. She met her husband in 1904, at the World's Fair where he offered to teach her the art of tattooing. He often tattooed his own artwork on her, and she was soon covered in ink. She was a circus sideshow act and often tattooed her circus coworkers. Although she did not invent tattooing as it was a custom in many Eastern cultures far before her time, she helped pave the way to normalize women having tattoos and becoming tattoo artists also.

Coloring page of a woman,
why must she desecrate the temple of her body?
Circus girl,
love a little quieter,
live in a duller color,
how closed minded they were.
I look at her, this woman
with more ink than skin,
her messy hair in a bun at the top of her head.
I am mesmerized.
She says to me,
some stories are better seen than heard.
They called it disgusting,
deplorable.
They averted their eyes,
looked at the grey ground,
the plain dust of it.
Would have rather looked at a blank page than me.
But I,
I never felt more like myself,
never felt more beautiful.
I didn't have to explain my worth,
I wore it on my body;
these arms, this chest,
my neck, bursting in color.
In the story of my life,
of love,
of laughter,
of art.

Queen Nanny Teaches Guerilla Warfare
Queen Nanny of the Maroons (1686-1733) was a military leader during the First Maroon War. She was very skilled in the guerrilla warfare that was carried out by her people against the British soldiers. She also passed down traditions, songs and customs to her people from their African ancestors to keep their culture alive and instill pride in their pasts. She led many of her people out of slavery to freedom and believed that a peace treaty with the British was another form of suppression.

Those white men,
who came in hoards,
taking our people from their homes,
children from their beds,
babies from their mother's wombs.
Who stacked us on top of one another,
set us out to sea.
Now those men speak of peace?
My heart has not known peace since Ghana;
my people will not know peace,
under these white thumbs.
Hold still child,
a bit of mud on the face,
dirt under the fingernails,
crouch down in the bushes,
and when they believe they are safe,
safe enough to rest,
safe enough to sleep,
attack.
Slit their throats,
bathe in your victory,
carry their empty bodies home,
place them on the pyre.
They will pay for their sins,
By keeping us warm.

Josephine Baker Teaches Singing

Josephine Baker (1906-1975) was a showgirl, activist, and spy during World War II. She began dancing at thirteen and worked her way up to Broadway. She was extravagant and even had a pet cheetah. She was such a huge influence in France and Europe overall that she began spying for the allies by socializing at high-level parties and carrying secret notes written in invisible ink on her music sheets across borders. When returning to America she became a civil rights leader alongside Martin Luther King Jr. and was the only official female speaker during the March on Washington. She also adopted twelve children of different ethnicities and they became known as the "rainbow tribe".

Black Pearl,
Bronze Venus,
Creole Goddess,
showgirl.
They begged for me,
for my melanin,
to enter the stage,
to let the wild out.
How easily they dismissed me,
when I was fully clothed,
without the glare of stage lights,
when I was just the woman at the party.
Spy girl,
used my own music to bring them down,
that's called harmonic warfare,
sing sweet dove,
sing the song of rebellion.
How different it was, returning home,
where I made my name,
now they were afraid to speak it.
So I stood,
I marched,
I spoke,
created my own tribe.
My rainbow of bodies,
this arc of love,
watch how it lights the whole sky.

Iva Toguiri Teaches Patriotism

Iva Toguiri (1916-2006) was a Japanese American broadcaster who got stuck in Japan while visiting a sick relative when the United States entered the second world war. While being held in Japan, she refused to give up her citizenship and was forced to present on an English language radio show, that promoted Japanese war propaganda and was meant to demoralize ally soldiers. When she returned to America she was interviewed by a reporter and indicted and tried for treason for giving aid and comfort to the enemy in a time of war. She was found guilty and spent 10 years in federal prison. After six years she was released for good behavior, and much later President Ford was finally convinced of her wrongful accusation and conviction and pardoned her for her crimes in 1977.

They called me Tokyo Rose,
but make no mistake I bleed stars and stripes.
Born in this country,
I was just in the wrong place at the wrong time.
Even as they held me,
tied me up at the wrists,
told me to give up my allied secrets,
I spat in their faces.
Sang America the Beautiful at the top of my lungs.
They harnessed my voice,
made me speak ill of my home,
those men who fought for it.
They claimed me as their own,
something they'd planted and cared for.
Back in my own soil,
after the guns had quieted,
when all that was left was shrapnel,
and the ringing in our ears,
they locked me up again.
For comforting the enemy,
for bringing peace to those who wanted us dead,
but I was being used,
just a pawn in their game.
They must not have known that,
surviving is a form of loyalty.

Marie-Madeline-Maguerite d'Aubray
Teaches Decision Making

Marie-Madeline-Maguerite d'Aubray (1630-1676) was a French noblewoman, tried and executed for poisoning numerous family members. After falling in love with a friend of her husband's, he was being sent away to prison by her father. She and her lover devised a plan to poison her family so that they could finally be together. However, by the time the plan was discovered her lover had died in prison and Marie was left to take responsibility on her own.

Perhaps it was a crime of passion.
Perhaps my girlish heart broke.
Or perhaps my girlish heart loved
more deeply, and fiercely,
than the heart of any man.
My life was chosen for me,
a common plight of my gender,
everything I would desire,
would be hand-picked by a man.
Father, husband, priest,
where was I?
So, when I found there was a wanting in me,
something unsanctioned by the men in my life,
I had to protect it. Had to save it.
My darling,
I don't know what I will do without you.
I wish there were a way for us to be together.
I am sorry for being what I am,
a woman who is not allowed to choose.
But there was a way,
unconventional, certainly;
unfeminine, most definitely;
but inhumane, perhaps not.
Perhaps my girlish heart was only choosing for them,
as they had for me.
Perhaps my womanly ways were only doing what was best,
for their fragile male bodies.

Ranavolona I Teaches Revolution

Ranavalona I (1778-1861) was ruler of Madagascar who is believed to have killed between 30-50% of her country's population. However, she also defeated both French and English armies and kept Madagascar independent from their rule. Her tactics were brutal, and the only real history left of her is told by the victors (the English and French) who eventually ruled after her death.

What is a queen with no children?
No husband?
Race them to the throne.
When they look shocked to see you,
sitting there,
divine as the day you were born,
smile.
Order them to fall on their swords.
This country,
your home,
where you live and rule,
they cannot have it.
Those white groping hands,
who take without asking,
touch without permission,
cut each finger,
slowly.
How beautiful you'll be,
sparkling in their pale jewels.

Christiana Edmunds Teaches Temperament
Christiana (1828-1907) was known as a spinster with a bit of an attitude. She began her life of crime when her boyfriend, a doctor in her town, wouldn't leave his wife for her. She cooked poison into a box of chocolates and delivered it to the woman. The doctor's wife survived the attack, but Christiana was identified for the crime. She attempted to kill others like this only succeeding by killing a young boy, though it is unclear if that was her intended target.

What a raw thing to be,
a woman enjoying the company of no one else.
How inventive of her to not want a man to whisk her away,
what novel gossip I was.
Such a lonely girl,
so ill-tempered,
like the hot, blood-coated breath of a wolf.
Like the whisper of a siren song,
the touch of the sweet thing that wants to kill you.
That's what I chose,
something sweet filled with poison.
They never can resist it when it's signed
with a note from their beloved.
So quick to stuff themselves full of love,
pretend it is from their husbands,
who left their beds so long ago.
And still they called me crazy.
Insane.
Maddened from unrequited love.
Driven to the edge by them,
and the sweet things they said,
the sweet things they'd wrapped their poison into.
If exposing them makes me ill-tempered,
perhaps I am.
But it didn't seem to bother them,
when they knelt before me,
begging for something sweet to get them by.

Leonarda Cianciulli Teaches Curse Breaking
Leonarda Cianciulli (1894-1970) was cursed by her mother to a life of misery after marrying a man she disapproved of. The curse seemed effective because Leonarda lost 13 of her 17 children. When Cianciulli began to fear for her son's life, as he was sent to war, she decided the only way to break the curse was human sacrifice. She found unmarried, unfamilied women and after killing them, chopped up their bodies and made them into soap or sometimes baked them into teacakes she shared with friends and family. Cianciulli would have presumably continued this pattern, but her son was accused of the murders, and she confessed to protect him.

It all started long before me,
the sins of the mother,
the mother's mother,
until you are staring at your ancestor.
Wondering how she could have been so selfish,
how could I have been so selfish?
So when I saw the solution,
standing in front of me,
in a dress,
and curls,
and no one to call home,
I did what had to be done.
And I served her to my guests,
So they could also taste,
what sweetness freedom holds.

Mary Anning Teaches Fossil Hunting

Mary Anning (1799-1847) grew up on what was called Jurassic Coast. She would collect what she called "curiosities", later known as fossils. Her first discovery was of a dolphin type reptile skull. Mary's discoveries however were rejected and sometimes stolen by the scientist community which was only men. She was never credited or recognized for her influence on the field until after her death.

We walk on a beach,
the sound of waves crashing,
and sand under our toes.
This plain woman speaks as she holds a stone in her hands.
These little curiosities.
My strange children.
I hold them in my hands,
sweet, crumbling bones.
They couldn't believe it,
didn't dare to think,
I could be strong enough to hold the bodies of dinosaurs.
To brush the dirt from their long, forgotten faces,
to care for them the way one cares for such discoveries.
They took them from me,
pried them from my hands,
whisked them away,
called them by new names.
I don't mind,
I know what they do not,
that all curiosities will eventually reach the shore.
That whoever finds those bones,
'The Curiosities of the Male Scientist',
that they should care for them,
tend to them,
love them.
The way all living things hope to one day be handled.

Marie Baker Teaches Using Your Assets

Marie Baker (unknown) also known as the Pretty Pants Bandit, was a robber who made headlines in 1933. She led a gang, of mostly women, in many hold ups where her calling card was to leave any hostages with their pants around their ankles. She was known as being very beautiful with deep brown eyes, and to always carry two guns. Most notably her arrest, when a hostage accidentally escaped while Marie checked her makeup in a nearby mirror.

Mama scolded my rouge,
detested my lipstick,
loathed my mascara.
Perhaps she feared I would be taken advantage of,
so I always took first.
What I wanted wasn't just money,
it was dignity.
I could smell it on them,
the way they looked at me,
drank me in like the street was a desert and I, the oasis.
What they wanted,
wafted off of them like fine cologne.
They thought if we went head-to-head
I'd be on the losing side.
They never anticipated it,
how hungry I was for winning.
So the next time you walk by a man,
and he smells of arrogance.
Look him in the eye,
bat your lashes,
take everything he has,
even the clothes on his back.
And before you leave him swimming in his own shame,
fix your lipstick.
Remind him he was so distracted by your pretty,
he didn't notice the guns in each hand,
until it was too late.

Sarah Good Teaches Spellcasting

Sarah Good (1653-1692) was the first woman accused of being a witch in Salem, Mass. She and her family were very poor and often stayed in other people's homes. She was arrested with two other women and eventually found guilty. She was to be hanged but it was postponed due to her pregnancy. Her newborn died in prison days before her execution and allegedly her final words were a curse to the reverend before her execution.

It was a simple life
and I was a simple woman.
Born to live,
but cursed to feel,
and condemned for a face.
Some women can hide,
can put on a smile,
and pretend there aren't any broken parts inside of them.
But inside of me was weather,
changing and unpredictable.
The shutters that were my ribs,
clanged against the windowpanes that were my lungs,
and the home that was my heart bruised too easily.
So I stood still in that church,
listened to them spit their hateful words,
held still under each damning gaze.
They asked me to speak, to explain,
and the storm inside of me tried.
The fire in me told them to look elsewhere.
But these locked up people do not speak in weather.
So with my final words I opened my mouth,
freed the hurricane, and promised that in their death,
what should be peaceful and gentle
for these God-fearing people,
would become an apocalypse.
And when their mouths fill with blood,
and glass stings their eyes,
in their final debilitating breath,
they will say my name.

Franceska Mann Teaches Balance

Franceska Mann (1917-1943) was a renowned ballerina and considered to be the most beautiful woman in Poland. In 1943 she was captured and taken to a concentration camp along with numerous other prisoners. When she realized their stop for "disinfection" was truly their death sentence by way of gas chamber, Mann began to distract the male guards by undressing slowly and seductively. When the men were close enough, she attacked, the other women followed Mann's lead and a riot began. In the end, the women did not overpower their captors and Mann ended her own life before the gas chamber was turned on.

When I was born,
I was wrapped in soft blankets.
My mother sang to me softly;
my father touched my cheek
like I would break at any moment.
How were they to know I would become so hard?
Perhaps it was when I danced,
tore up my feet,
balanced my body weight on one toe.
They'd tried to cage me like a small, helpless bird.
They didn't know I was a lioness,
and that lions live in packs.
So when they're cornered,
trapped, in huddled masses,
afraid, shaking, cold
under the hunter's self-righteous gaze,
they do not lie down,
do not give up.
They sharpen their claws,
bare their teeth,
and pounce.

Olympe de Gouges Teaches Activism

Olympe de Gouges (1748-1793) was a Frenchwoman, abolitionist and feminist who was executed for abandoning the cares of her household to be involved in politics. Olympe was outspoken about equal rights for women, people of color and people of lower class in France. After her death her home was raided, and all of her papers were burnt. It wasn't until decades after her death that a historian found proof of her existence. She even wrote about how, after her death, men would erase her from history; she hoped to be rediscovered post-mortem and celebrated by other women.

Such a sly, selfish snake.
Pampered, petty, princess.
My arrogant mouth,
this wicked tongue,
this vicious mind.
How could I know the struggle of womanhood?
Who was I to understand the curse
of being a second priority to your own body?
Perhaps I should have stopped,
sewn my own mouth closed,
cut out my tongue and served it to them on a platter.
When you are a woman who dares to ask for more,
you become a cautionary tale,
of the gluttony of educated women.
Men will try to erase you,
drain your body of blood and thirst for more.
Use your bones as toothpicks,
and fuss over all of the you still stuck in their gums.
They will burn your home to ash,
and make you sweep up the mess.
They will want to own you.
And perhaps they will.
Shove you inside some dusty cupboard,
beside childhood toys and other forgotten artifacts.
They will have children,
who will have children,
who will have children,
who will find you,

covered in cobwebs,
heart beating an uneven symphony.
Tell them your story,
how their father's, father's, father tried in vain to quiet you.
tell them about the megaphone that is their own throats,
tell them the work is not finished,
that there is more to be done.
Only then will you rest,
drift away into the nothingness of space,
a smile still on your greedy lips.

Good Advice from Bad Women

Annette Kellerman Teaches Marine Biology
Annette Kellerman (1886-1975) was an Australian swimmer, aquatic performer and actress. In her adulthood she set many records and performed as a mermaid. She attempted to swim across the Chanel three times and after succeeding in her final attempt, she retired from long distance swimming. She was arrested for wearing a short one-piece swimsuit and made national news; most swimsuits for women were long pants. She performed all of her own water stunts and is credited with making women's swimming socially acceptable.

She looks at me,
flips her tail in the shining water,
her laugh is a siren song.
She tells me,
*Across all of the blue,
in the deep waters,
where the waves are near black.
There is an island,
where doubt cannot breathe,
the sand is soft as your baby blanket.
When the wind blows,
it sounds like your mother's lullaby,
or your father's warbling whistle.
Every tree blooms with fruit,
and there is a stream of ambrosia running by.
The only way to the island however,
is through fear,
and heartbreak,
and self loathing.
You must battle monsters,
with names like Jealousy, Greed and Time.
You must swim until your arms scream,
and further still.
The true evils,
stand behind you,
on the shore you must leave;
they fill you with rocks and disappointment and anger.
You must shed them before you can float.*

But them,
the enemies,
the naysayers,
they don't know how to swim.
How to always move forward,
to adapt,
to shed what is not useful.
So swim on,
push and push,
until there is not more in you,
and push some more.
Because that is how girls,
become sharks.

Junko Tabei Teaches Rock Climbing
Junko Tabei (1939-2016) was a mountaineer who formed the first all-female ascent to Annapurna III in Nepal. She also made history as the first woman in history to scale Everest at age 35, with a toddler at home. She made history again by being the first female to climb the highest peaks on each of the seven continents. She was vocal about environmentalism and keeping mountain ranges clean of debris from climbing teams.

In the city,
there is so much noise.
Smog and smoke fill the air,
deteriorating the throats of the birds,
who owned this sky before us;
who will own it after.
In the city,
there is no peace.
Honking cars and radio waves,
so much chatter.
But on the mountain,
there is only quiet.
Between myself, the rock, and the sky,
there is only one breath.
On the hard packed ice,
only one beating heart.
We grew together,
the mountain and I.
Each in our own ways,
sprouting new life each spring,
and shedding the old each autumn.
The mountain and I,
warriors.
The rock and I,
partners.
The Earth and I,
goddesses.
Do not be afraid
to seek higher ground.
It is where the perspective is clearest.

Timoclea Teaches Repercussions

Timoclea (4th Century BCE) was a servant to a military captain under Alexander the Great. He often ordered her to bring him food and wine and raped her. After the attack he refused to leave; he was convinced she'd hidden all of her riches somewhere and eventually she said she'd take him to her hiding spot. Instead she lured him to a dry well and pushed him in. She began to throw rocks at her attacker until he was fully buried. When his body was discovered, she was taken to Alexander the Great where she confessed to everything, defiantly. Instead of punishing her for her crime, Alexander the Great apologized for what had happened to her, let her go free and made sure all of his other soldiers knew she and her family were to be respectfully left alone, and that no crimes like this, by his military men, would be allowed under his rule.

They marched on us in daylight;
the sun was still high in the sky.
I can still feel the heat on my cheek.
He took me in the moonlight,
my scream was the loudest animal call.
I can still feel his hand over my mouth.
When he asked for more,
to take all I had left,
It was my turn.
My turn to take.
From inside the well,
his cavern of sin,
he looked so small.
With the sky lifted above my head,
I felt big.
Bigger than him,
than his armies,
than his emperor.
I did not apologize.
I did not regret.
The heat would not redden my cheeks,
he would not bruise my skin,
I was done being pushed without pushing back.

Author Profile

Carly Herriges is a recent graduate of Falmouth University with a degree in journalism and creative writing.

She is a paraprofessional at an elementary school, but writing is her dream. As well as poetry she writes fiction and fantasy.

This is her first published book, and she is thrilled to share it with readers.

www.ingramcontent.com/pod-product-compliance
Lightning Source LLC
Chambersburg PA
CBHW062148100526
44589CB00014B/1746